Caring and Sharing

Activities for 3–5 Year Olds

Linda Mort and
Janet Morris

Brilliant
PUBLICATIONS

We hope you enjoy using this book. If you would like further information on other titles published by Brilliant Publications, please write to the address given below or look on our website: www.brilliantpublications.co.uk.

Other books in the Activities for 3–5 Year Olds series:

All About Us	Pets
Colours	Shopping
Families	Water
Food	Weather
Gardening	

Published by Brilliant Publications,
Unit 10, Sparrow Hall Farm, Edlesborough, Bedfordshire, LU6 2ES
website: www.brilliantpublications.co.uk

Written by Linda Mort and Janet Morris
Second edition revised and updated in 2012 by Debbie Chalmers
Illustrated by Kirsty Wilson

Printed ISBN 978 0 85747 660 9
ebook ISBN 978 0 85747 022 5

The Publisher accepts no responsibility for accidents arising from the activities described in this book.

First published in 1997, second edition 2012
10 9 8 7 6 5 4 3 2 1

Contents

To avoid the clumsy 'he/she', the child is referred to throughout as 'she'.

Introduction

'Caring and sharing' is a very simple phrase to which young childen readily respond. If this approach to interacting and living with others is introduced in a positive and enjoyable way, and followed from an early enough age, it can enhance a child's learning potential and personal skills and build a firm foundation for later life.

The activities in this book take into account the three characteristics of effective learning: playing and exploring, active learning, and creating and thinking critically. They encourage families to become involved, so that the adults at home and those in the early years settings may work together consistently to support the children's developing skills and values. They include ideas for encouraging children to enjoy using the words 'please' and 'thank you', to take turns, to share and to listen and speak to each other courteously. Children will learn to appreciate kindness in others and to show care and respect for members of their own families, friends and others in the community.

The activities are linked to the Early Learning Goals of the Department for Education's revised *Statutory Framework for the Early Years Foundation Stage* (September 2012), and its guidance document, *Development Matters*. They respect the children's developing skills, abilities and self-images and encourage them to form positive relationships with each other and with the adults in their setting, as well as with their families at home.

Children learn through playing and exploring, creating and thinking critically. The role of an early years practitioner is to provide stimulating and challenging activities within an enabling environment. Ideas must be flexible enough to meet the needs of each individual as a unique child and to build upon the children's knowledge and interests to promote active learning. All of the activities in this book may be easily adapted to suit individual children or groups of any size.

The book uses materials which are likely to be readily available within your class or group's location, or which can be easily provided by the children's families or carers, if requested.

'Please' and 'thank you' bubbles

Learning opportunities
* Developing an awareness and an understanding of when and why the words 'please' and 'thank you' should be used in conversation

Links to the Early Learning Goals
* Communication and language – Listening and attention, Speaking

Also

* Personal, social and emotional development – Making relationships

Equipment and resources
Card, felt-tipped pen, scissors, drinking straw, sticky tape, play-people, miniature 'props' (eg furniture, small toys, 'shopping' items, etc), comics showing speech bubbles.

Activity
Make a card 'speech bubble', showing 'Please' on one side, and 'Thank you' on the reverse. Attach a drinking straw to make a flag. Show the children the speech bubbles in comics. Invite the children to help their play-people to say 'please' and 'thank you' using the special 'speech bubble'. Give the speech bubble to one child and ask whether he could 'twirl' the 'bubble' to show the right word, whenever you use the words 'please' and 'thank you'. (Remember that

'please' and 'thank you' are not as prominent in some other languages and cultures and some children may be unused to using them. Respect this as you explain that the words are used in British culture and learning to use them appropriately will be beneficial to all children living in the United Kingdom.)

Select two play-people and a 'prop', and make up a very simple dialogue in which one play-person uses 'please' and the other 'thank you' (eg a child in bed, asking a parent for a drink). Suggest that children make up dialogues, in turn, asking the child next to them to 'twirl' the 'bubble' to fit the speech.

Extension

Each child could make a 'please and thank you bubble' to take home. If parents know that these words are being practised in the setting, they may be supportive in emphasizing them at home too and in keeping practitioners informed of the children's progress. Share this feedback with the children and praise them for making an effort.

Discussion

Ask children if they can think of particular people who speak politely as a part of their job, such as bus drivers ('Tickets, please!'), or dentists ('Open wide, please!'), or those serving in shops or banks ('Thank you for waiting'). Ask them to think about how it feels if people do not say 'thank you'.

That's just like...

Learning opportunities
* Understanding and empathizing with characters in stories

Links to the Early Learning Goals
* Communication and language – Listening and attention

Also
* Expressive arts and design – Being imaginative

Equipment and resources
Stories (in books or made up) about experiencing kindness from others, percussion instruments.

Activity
Choose key points from the story for the children to act out, perhaps to the accompaniment of percussion instruments. Change the characters and the setting. For example, if the story is about a child who is new to a playgroup, and feels lonely at first, the children could pretend to be a little squirrel who finds himself in a new forest, without any friends. Include one strong descriptive detail that also occurs in the story. For example, if in the story the little boy felt especially sad at playtime when it started to rain and all the other children ran inside, laughing, the squirrel could be feeling especially sad, lonely, shivering and cold when it starts to rain, and all the other squirrels dart off together, laughing to find shelter.

A few hours later tell or read the actual story. Do
not mention the earlier 'squirrel' experience. Let the
children make their own connections.

Extension
Ask the children to talk about stories which reminded
them of themselves, or people they know.

Discussion
Chat with the children about when they feel sad,
who cheers them up and how they manage to do it.
Encourage them to offer ideas on how they can be
kind to people and cheer them up or make sure they
don't feel sad.

Forgetful Ferdinand

Learning opportunities

* Listening to, understanding and following instructions for a game involving physical activities

Links to the Early Learning Goals

* Communication and language – Understanding

Also

* Physical development – Moving and handling

Equipment and resources

A space for the children.

Activity

An adult can take on the role of 'Forgetful Ferdinand', who often forgets to say 'please'. Give the children instructions to follow, as in 'Simon says', but for all actions you wish them to follow, say 'Ferdinand says please …'. The children must not carry out any instruction which does not include the word 'please'. This is a good activity to help develop awareness, eg 'Ferdinand says please stand behind your chair' or 'Ferdinand says please sit under the climbing frame'.

Extension

Extend the game to a shopping context by playing
'Ferdinand forgets to say thank you!', with Ferdinand
asking to buy something from the 'shopkeeper'.
Initiate some role-play with the children, involving
adults and children playing the parts of Ferdinand
and his shopkeepers. Pretend that Ferdinand always
forgets to say 'thank you' and so the shopkeepers
take the items back again and ask 'What do you say?'
Ferdinand could ask for reminders from others in the
group when he forgets what to say.

Discussion

Ask the children to think of anyone they know who
sometimes forgets to say 'please' and 'thank you',
such as a younger brother or sister whom they could
help to teach.

Can I help you?

Learning opportunities
* Developing and improving skills and abilities in dressing and undressing independently and manipulating fasteners
* Working together and helping each other to solve practical problems

Links to the Early Learning Goals
* Physical development – Health and self-care
Also
* Personal, social and emotional development – Making relationships

Equipment and resources
Children's outdoor clothing (eg coats, anoraks, gloves, scarves, hats, etc).

Activity
Make time before an outing or going outside to play for children to practise putting on their own outdoor clothes. Suggest that they all gather their coats and hats, etc. Encourage them to work hard at putting on their clothes independently, and, instead of asking an adult for help if they cannot fasten a zip or a button, to ask another child for help. Support the whole group to ensure that each child has an opportunity to both give and receive help.

Extension

Make a pictogram (a bar chart with pictures) showing how many children have coats with buttons, compared with those with zips or press studs. You could also make a pictogram to compare numbers of gloves and mittens.

Discussion

Ask the children to decide which types of clothes are the most difficult to put on. Suggest that they put one hand on top of one of their gloves and match each of their fingers to a glove finger, or do the same thing with a mitten, 'bunching up' four fingers together. Offer strategies for telling a right boot or shoe from a left one. (Suggest that, if they put them side by side and the toes are pointing away from each other, then the shoes 'don't want to be friends' and are the wrong way round. Explain that buckles or velcro fastenings must be on the outsides of the shoes, because, if they touch each other on the insides, they will stick together and we will not be able to walk.)

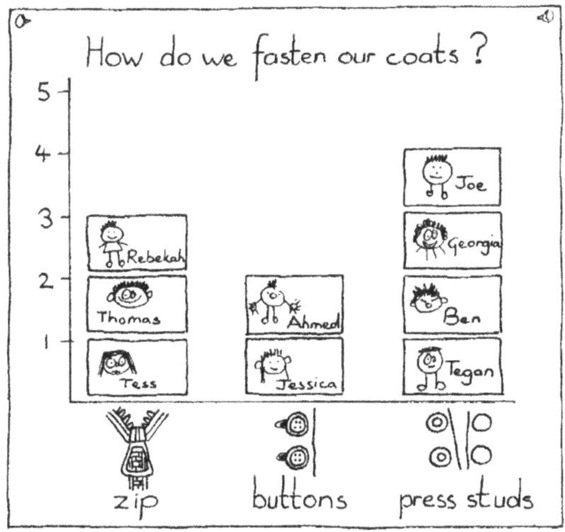

'Excuse me!' and 'Sorry!'

Learning opportunities
* Developing and improving skills and confidence in riding a tricycle
* Developing spatial awareness and an understanding of how to move safely and carefully within a group or between obstacles

Links to the Early Learning Goals
* Physical development – Moving and handling
Also
* Personal, social and emotional development – Managing feelings and behaviour

Equipment and resources
A large space, a group of six children, a firefighter's helmet, a police cap or helmet, an ambulance worker's cap, five chairs placed one behind each other in a row with plenty of space between, one tricycle.

Activity
Invite five children to sit on the chairs and pretend to be 'traffic driving along'. Ask a sixth child whether she would like to be the driver of a fire engine, a police car or an ambulance and offer her the appropriate hat to wear. Encourage her to ride the tricycle, weaving in and out of the chairs to 'overtake', using a 'siren voice', repeating the expression 'excuse me! excuse me! excuse me!' (instead of 'der… der! der… der! der… der!'). If the tricycle touches a chair, the emergency driver must say 'sorry!'. The children

should take turns to be the emergency driver and the
'traffic vehicles'.

Extension

Ask five children to stand one behind the other,
with a space between each child. Tell the children to
pretend that they have very heavy shopping bags
and have stopped for a moment to have a little rest.
Invite a sixth child to pretend to be in a hurry and to
rush between the standing children, saying 'excuse
me!' as she passes between each pair. If she touches a
standing child, she should say 'sorry!'

Discussion

Tell the children that a siren on an emergency vehicle
means: 'Excuse me, I'm in a hurry, please let me pass!'.
Talk about how drivers of emergency vehicles often
need to drive very quickly, but that they always take
care not to crash into any other traffic. Explain that if
emergency vehicles or any traffic do bump into each
other, then everyone is very sorry indeed.

Caring and sharing week

Learning opportunities
* Sharing personal possessions and taking care when using the possessions of others
* Taking turns and sharing ideas with friends

Links to the Early Learning Goals
* Personal, social and emotional development – Managing feelings and behaviour, Making relationships

Equipment and resources
Forms that parents and carers can use to record children's 'caring and sharing' behaviour at home and return to the setting for practitioners to use with the group.

Activity
Suggest to parents and carers that each child might bring a toy or game from home to share with the other children during 'Caring and sharing week'. Ask for the item to be labelled with the child's name and preferably not to have too many small parts. During the week, encourage each child to explain how to use her item. Encourage the children to ask politely for a 'turn' (see also 'In five minutes', page 34), and to use each other's toys carefully.

Extension

Offer a form to each child's parent or carer and suggest that they write down any special 'caring and sharing' or kind behaviour that their child displays at home and return the form to the setting during the 'Caring and sharing week'. The information on the forms can be read by all the practitioners and noted by each child's key person, then shared with the children during group and circle times. An event could be arranged for the end of the special week, to which families and carers are invited, allowing children and practitioners to describe and display the work and activities that they have enjoyed and learned from.

Discussion

Talk about how much fun and how interesting it can be to share our belongings with others and how other people can give us new ideas for using them. Ask the children which toys they share with their friends when they come to visit. Encourage them to think about what would happen, and how everyone would feel, if children did not share their toys when they played together.

Word traffic

Learning opportunities
* Taking turns to speak and to listen within a small, familiar group

Links to the Early Learning Goals
* Personal, social and emotional development – Self-confidence and self-awareness, Making relationships

Also
* Communication and language – Speaking
* Mathematics - Numbers

Equipment and resources
A set of numbers (one each), card, saucer, felt-tipped pen, scissors, orange, green and red paper, glue, sticky tape, police cap or helmet.

Activity
Cut one saucer-sized circle out of card per child. Stick orange paper on one side and green paper on the other side. Cut out one larger circle and make this red on both sides. Give each child a number and a circle, to put on the table in front of them. The circles should be 'orange' side up. Tell the children that, when someone is talking in a group, they must listen to one another and not interrupt. The child who is speaking may turn her circle over to show the green side. Everyone else must listen and think about what they might like to say when it is their turn. They should not speak, but

be 'getting ready' (like a car at traffic lights). When a child's turn comes, she may turn her circle over to show the green side and may then speak.

Invite children to take turns to be a police officer, wearing the cap or helmet and holding the large red circle. The 'police officer' must hold up the red circle to stop any children who interrupt.

An adult can begin a discussion, then invite the child with the number 1 to turn her circle over to show the green side and say something, followed by the child with number 2 and then number 3.

Extension

Once the children are used to taking turns, try without the numbers. Emphasize that everyone will get a turn!

Discussion

Encourage the children to remember what happens when everyone tries to talk at once. Ask them to imagine what would happen to traffic if there were no traffic lights.

'Come aboard'

Learning opportunities
* Working cooperatively as a member of a group or team
* Using a large construction set to build a large model of a bus

Links to the Early Learning Goals
* Personal, social and emotional development – Making relationships

Also
* Physical development – Moving and handling

Equipment and resources
Large construction set with nuts, bolts and wheels, paper, felt-tipped pens or pencils, sticky tape.

Activity
This activity works best with a group of five or six children. Ask the children to work together to create a bus for a special trip to the seaside. Encourage them to practise screwing in and unscrewing the nuts and bolts. Ask each child to be in charge of one particular part of the construction set, such as nuts or bolts, wheels or cubes, so that the children have to work cooperatively by asking each other for the parts they need. When the bus is finished, the children can draw their faces with felt-tipped pens on squares of paper to represent faces at the windows and attach them with sticky tape.

Extension

Sing 'The Wheels on the Bus' song changing the words to include individual children, eg 'Lauren on the bus has a sister called Isabel….'

Discussion

Tell the children how, in car and bus factories, people work together in 'teams', all helping one another. Talk about sports teams, such as football teams, where the players have to kick the ball to one another and not keep the ball to themselves.

Thank you!

Learning opportunities
* Increasing skills and confidence in writing for a purpose

Links to the Early Learning Goals
* Literacy – Writing

Equipment and resources
Paper, envelopes, stamps, felt-tipped pens, crayons, pencils, collage materials, glue, scissors.

Activity
Encourage children to think of people who could be thanked for their kindness and help – both those known personally to the children and others. Support the children as they write cards or letters, using their own level of emergent writing, or with a 'scribe', if necessary. For example, one child could write a thank you card to granny, for taking him kite flying, or a group of children could make a giant card to say thank you to the cleaners or the caretaker or the person who delivers the post. Take the children out to post their letters or arrange for the children to give them to the people concerned.

Extension

Suggest to children that they pretend to be characters
from stories or or rhymes and write 'thank you' letters
to people who were kind to them, updating their
'benefactors' with details of what happened to them
after their meeting! Examples could be: Cinderella
to the Fairy Godmother, Jack to the Giant's wife, and
Humpty to 'all the King's horses and men' who tried
to help him.

Discussion

Encourage children to talk about other ways of saying
'thank you' to people. For example, they could choose
to give hugs or kisses to families and friends, or to
make presents or offer to do good deeds for people
they know less well.

The caring and sharing alphabet

Learning opportunities
* Linking sounds to letters
* Naming and sounding letters of the alphabet
* Developing vocabulary and imagination on a 'caring and sharing' theme

Links to the Early Learning Goals
* Literacy – Reading
Also
* Expressive arts and design – Being imaginative

Equipment and resources
An alphabet frieze, a set of alphabet letters, a drawstring bag.

Activity
Place the alphabet letters in the bag and invite one child to choose a letter, say its sound and stand by the matching letter on the frieze. (The frieze could be laid on the floor.) Support the child as she makes up a very simple 'caring and sharing' story involving the alphabet picture. For example, **a** – 'I shared my **apple** with my sister'; **b** – 'I let my friend play with my new **ball**'; **n** – 'The **nurse** made the little girl feel better'; **z** – 'The **zebra** picked up her friend when he fell in the mud', etc.

Extension

Suggest to the children that they bring in their own alphabet books from home and make up 'caring and sharing' stories about the pictures contained in them.

Discussion

Talk about the animals and toys that appear in the pictures on the frieze. Ask children who might look after the animals. Discuss whether they have any toys that are similar to those shown on the frieze. Chat about sharing the toys and who gave them as presents.

A handful of rings

Learning opportunities

* Understanding and practising the sharing out of items equally between two people

Links to the Early Learning Goals

* Mathematics – Numbers

Equipment and resources

Plates, hoop-like crisps (you will need ten per child).

Activity

Children must wash their hands thoroughly, under supervision, before taking part in this activity. Ask the children to sit on the floor, in pairs, facing one another, with a plate of ten 'hoops' between them. One child should hold up her outstretched fingers on one hand. The other child, 'the sharing child', should also hold up the fingers of one free hand. With the other hand, she may pick up the 'hoops', one at a time, and slide one onto one finger of her partner's hand, then one onto one finger of her 'free' hand, saying each time, 'one for you, one for me', until all ten 'hoops' are used up. The pair may then eat the 'hoops'. You should now replace the ten 'hoops', after which the other child can become the 'sharing' child.

Extension

Make a picture frieze of six hands for the wall, showing the progression from an empty hand with 'no' hoops, to a hand with five 'hoops'. Encourage children to match the numbers 0, 1, 2, 3, 4, 5 to the pictures.

Discussion

Ask the children if they have noticed their parents sharing out the food when friends and relations visit. Talk about giving one item to each person or trying to cut a cake to make pieces of the same size for everyone.

One peach each

Learning opportunities
* Developing an understanding of sharing out items, so that people can have one each

Links to the Early Learning Goals
* Mathematics – Numbers

Equipment and resources
One fresh peach, one plastic plate, red and yellow powder paints, clear varnish, one die, one hoop, salt dough. *(Salt dough can be made by mixing the following ingredients together to make a firm dough: 3 cups plain flour, 2 cups salt, 4 teaspoons wallpaper paste (without fungicide), 1 $^1/_3$ cups water. If more water is needed, add one drop at a time, kneading as you go.)*

Activity
Show the children a fresh peach and then help them to make a quantity of pretend 'peaches' from salt dough. Bake in a very cool oven (70-100°C) for a minimum of 12 hours, turning occasionally. When the 'peaches' are cool, encourage the children to paint them and then an adult should varnish them. Place the 'peaches' on a plate on the floor inside the hoop. One child throws the die and asks the corresponding number of children to sit around the circle. The child must then share out the 'peaches' one each. (Note: make sure the children know that these are 'pretend peaches' and that they should not be eaten.)

Extension

Before each child shares the 'peaches', put differing amounts of 'peaches' on the plate and ask the child to estimate whether there will be 'enough' for 'one each'. Suggest to more able or confident children that they could give 'two each' and ask if they can tell how many children they should invite to share in that case.

Discussion

Ask children to discuss whether it would be fair for one child to keep all of the peaches, or for some children to have more than others. Encourage them to offer ideas of what to do with any 'left over' peaches.

Make a queue and we'll get through

Learning opportunities
* Counting skills, placing numbers in order and counting forward and back
* Understanding the concept and usefulness of a queue to promote safety and fairness

Links to the Early Learning Goals
* Mathematics – Numbers

Also

* Personal, social and emotional development – Managing feelings and behaviour

Equipment and resources
Five play-people, three kitchen roll tubes, masking tape, scissors.

Activity
Make a narrow 'door-frame', using three kitchen roll tubes, cut to size. Secure the tubes using masking tape, and fix the 'door-frame' to a table, again with masking tape. Arrange the play-people side by side in a row in front of the 'door', and demonstrate that they cannot fit through the door all at once, when they are 'side by side'. Show that if they make a queue, 'one behind the other', then they will all get through the door. Keep counting the play-people, when they are side by side and when they are one behind the other and point out

that there are always five play-people and that they
will all get through the door eventually.

Extension

Repeat the activity by gathering a group of children
beside a doorway and asking how they can all get
through. Encourage them to organize themselves into
a queue, but first say with them, 'Make a queue and
we'll get through!'

Discussion

Remind the children of how many play people want
to get through the doorway and let them see that
they cannot all get through if they are side by side.
Ask what would happen if they tried to do this and
how they can stop themselves from getting hurt.
Encourage children to count how many of themselves
are in a queue waiting to go through the doorway and
to decide whether they will all be able to go through,
whether it matters who goes first and why not.

Giant piggy bank

Learning opportunities
* Understanding the concept of saving money as a group in order to buy an item that can be shared by everyone

Links to the Early Learning Goals
* Mathematics – Shape, space and measures

Equipment and resources
A large plastic bottle, sharp scissors, a pipe cleaner, card, felt-tipped pens, pretend money, sticky tape, educational suppliers' catalogue, collection of piggy banks and money boxes.

Activity
Show the collection of piggy banks and money boxes to the children and talk about 'saving up' to buy something special. Decide with the children on a special toy or item which could be bought by everyone, to share. Choose the item from one of the catalogues. Make a piggy bank by cutting a pig's face and legs from the card and sticking them on to the bottle. Cut a slot in the top for the coins and a larger flap underneath, through which the coins can be retrieved, which can be taped shut until needed. Add a curly tail made from a pipe cleaner. Encourage the children to fill the piggy bank with pretend money and to notice how much more money is raised if everyone contributes.

Ideally, arrange for the chosen toy or item to be ordered as soon as possible. (Be aware that, if you have Muslim children and their families within your group, they will be offended by this reference to pigs and so you will need to substitute another animal.)

Extension

Whenever you are asking for donations from children and families to raise money for a charity or good cause, invite them to put the coins into the transparent piggy bank and watch the amount grow.

Discussion

Ask the children who the toys in the setting belong to and who looks after them. Remind them of how to share and make sure that toys do not get lost or broken.

In five minutes

Learning opportunities
* Developing a sense of how long 'five minutes' is
* Understanding fairness and waiting patiently for a turn

Links to the Early Learning Goals
* Mathematics – Shape, space and measures

Equipment and resources
A plastic fronted wall clock with a clear face, a decorative plate-stand, coloured peel-off labels.

Activity
Stand the clock upright in the plate-stand and keep it in a place that is known and accessible to the children. Whenever one child wishes to use something being used by someone else, encourage the child to ask for a 'turn', and for the second child to say 'yes, in five minutes'. The first child should then bring the clock to you. Point out the 'big hand', and the next number it will move to, after five minutes. Place a coloured label by this number. The child may now take the clock and stand it up nearby, 'keeping an eye' on the time.

Extension

Use a three-minute egg timer once or twice to enable
the children to appreciate how it feels to wait for a
turn for three or six minutes.

Discussion

Share ideas with the children of things they could
do while waiting for three, five or six minutes, such
as looking at a book, playing with another toy or
sweeping up some sand.

Baby's bottle time

Learning opportunities

* Developing an awareness and some understanding of volume and capacity

Links to the Early Learning Goals

* Mathematics – Shape, space and measures

Equipment and resources

Babies feeding bottles, selection of baby dolls, jugs, cling film, white powder paint, water.

Activity

Mix a quantity of thin white powder paint, to represent 'milk'. (Explain to the children that this is 'pretend milk' and that people should not drink it.) Pour the 'milk' into jugs and let the children carefully fill the bottles for their 'babies', trying not to spill any 'milk'. Ask them to guess how many bottles they can fill with the 'milk' in the jug. When the 'feeds' are ready, use cling film and the bottles' discs before adding the teats to prevent the 'milk' leaking from the bottles.

Extension

Provide resources for children to have a dolls' tea party. Fill 'milk' jugs with powder-paint milk and tea pots with cold tea. Invite the children to put the 'milk' in the cups either before or after the 'tea'.

Remind the children to estimate when they should stop pouring the tea or milk to try to avoid the cups overflowing.

Discussion

Talk about the need to look after babies and to feed them carefully. Explain to the children that some babies drink milk from their mothers and some from bottles. Talk about how babies of different sizes and weights need different amounts of milk, and how sometimes they will drink a whole bottle and sometimes only half. Draw the children's attention to the marks and measurements on the bottles which indicate how many ounces or millilitres of milk the baby has drunk.

Shopping for baby

Learning opportunities
* Matching and counting skills
* Simple addition
* Considering the needs and preferences of friends and family members

Links to the Early Learning Goals
* Mathematics – Numbers

Also
* Understanding the world – People and communities

Equipment and resources
A large number of baby items (eg bottles, baby clothes, baby shampoo, boxes of wet wipes, rattles, nappies, etc), large piece of card, felt-tipped pen, pretend money, baby doll, baby catalogue and glue (optional).

Activity
On a large piece of card draw a picture of each baby item (or cut and paste pictures from a catalogue). Write the price alongside. Choose one child to be the mummy or daddy, complete with new 'baby'. Ask the other children to be big 'brothers' and 'sisters', helping to buy items for the new baby from the baby shop. Help the children to match the item they wish to buy with the picture or drawing on the card. Support children as they count how many bottles they have bought, or how many rattles, and then encourage

them to add up the different items and to count how many items altogether.

Extension

Change the items in the shop and go shopping for Christmas and birthday presents for relations and friends. Ask the children to think about what their relatives and friends like doing and what they might like for a present.

Discussion

Ask children to suggest ways in which they could help to look after a new baby. Talk with them about the toys they might buy if they had a new baby in their family.

Isn't that kind?

Learning opportunities
* Speaking confidently within a familiar group
* Describing the actions of family members from first-hand experience and memory

Links to the Early Learning Goals
* Understanding the world – People and communities

Equipment and resources
Photographs of children's families.

Activity
Gather the children together and invite them to sit in a group or a circle. Encourage them to take turns to stand, holding up photographs of their family, or the people they live with, for everyone to see. Ask each child to think of one kind action that her daddy, mummy, brother or sister performs for her and one that she performs in return. For example, her big brother might help her to tie her shoelaces and she might help him by fetching his coat.

Extension

Make little concertina booklets entitled 'Being kind'
with the photograph the child has brought in on the
front cover. The children can illustrate the pages with
alternating pictures of the child being kind to a family
member and a family member being kind to the child.
Support the children in writing captions to go with
their illustrations, acting as a scribe if necessary.

Discussion

Encourage the children to chat about what actions or
behaviours make members of their families pleased
with them, so that they smile, or call them 'good girl'
or 'good boy'.

I can help you

Learning opportunities
* Developing an awareness of different adult occupations and, in particular, the 'caring professions'

Links to the Early Learning Goals
* Understanding the world – People and communities

Equipment and resources
Pictures of people or animals needing help (eg a cat stuck in a tree, a child who has fallen off a bicycle, a child who is crying because she is lost in a crowd of adults), a firefighter's helmet, a nurse's hat, a police officer's cap or helmet, chairs, a source of music.

Activity
Attach the pictures to the wall, a few feet apart, within the children's reach. Ask three children at a time to dance around to the music wearing one of the hats. When the music stops, each child may go to the picture of their choice and say, 'I can help you'. Encourage the children to explain in more detail how they would help the animal or the person in the picture.

Extension

Tell the classic tale of 'The Lion and the Mouse' in which the Lion first saves the Mouse's life and the Mouse is later able to help the Lion by gnawing through the hunter's rope. Explain that the story shows how we can all help each other in some way, however small.

Discussion

Ask whether any of the children have had contact with a nurse, a police officer or a firefighter, or with anyone else who helped them or their families. Encourage them to describe how they were helped.

Shadow puppets

Learning opportunities
* Creating a puppet show, using a screen, a lamp and other props
* Empathizing with characters in nursery rhymes who hurt themselves and are helped by others

Links to the Early Learning Goals
* Understanding the world – Technology
Also
* Communication and language – Listening and attention
* Expressive arts and design – Being imaginative

Equipment and resources
A screen made out of a piece of white sheet fastened to a one metre square frame of wood or stiff card, a large torch or lamp, cut-out card nursery rhyme characters and props (attached to the end of rulers or dowelling sticks), chairs.

Activity
Encourage children to set up the equipment for the puppet show and the chairs for the audience and then to take turns to operate the lamp or the puppets or to watch the show. The lamp operator needs to shine the light on the back of the screen. Holding up the cut-out characters behind the screen will make them appear as shadows on the screen. Adults and children can take on the roles of different nursery rhyme characters needing help. For example, Humpty Dumpty could

fall off the wall and the children could suggest ways of helping, eg gluing him back together.

Extension

The children could act out the nursery rhymes improvising their own solutions. For example, Jack might be taken to hospital in an ambulance rather than having his head wrapped in vinegar and brown paper.

Discussion

Talk with the children about which nursery rhyme characters need help from other people and what they do to help. Ask them who helps them when they fall over or hurt themselves, whether they feel upset and what makes them feel better.

Grow a green pepper plant

Learning opportunities

* Understanding how to grow a plant from a seed and the conditions that plants need for healthy growth

Links to the Early Learning Goals

* Understanding the world – The world

Equipment and resources

Plastic cups, potting compost, green peppers, sharp knife, water, peel off labels, felt-tipped pen, plastic spoons.

Activity

Demonstrate how to fill a cup with compost, using a spoon, and support children in putting in an appropriate amount. Stick a name label on each cup. Cut the green peppers in half and let the children remove the seeds. Ask each child to sprinkle a few seeds on the compost. Add a top layer of compost and then a little water. (Note: the children should avoid touching their faces during this activity and wash their hands throughly afterwards, as pepper seeds can sometimes cause irritation if they come into contact with the eyes or the mouth.)

Encourage the children to take the cups home, but remind them (and parents/carers) to keep the compost moist. The seeds will start to grow in a matter of days and luxuriant plants will appear in a few weeks. Ask the children to bring their plants back to show everyone.

Extension

Let the children try planting red or yellow pepper seeds too.

Discussion

Explain how we need to feel the compost each day to see if the plant needs watering. Talk about why the plant needs light to help it grow.

Share a bath!

Learning opportunities
* Developing an awareness and an understanding of the importance of not wasting water, as part of caring for the environment

Links to the Early Learning Goals
* Understanding the world – The world

Equipment and resources
Two dolls, two baby baths, bubble bath, waterproof aprons, large jug, face cloths, towels.

Activity
Ask the children to undress the dolls ready for a bath. Place one bath and a jug of warm water in front of the children. Give the children a problem to solve. Tell them: 'We don't want to waste water as it is precious, but we do want to bath both dolls.' Ask them what they think you should do. Most children will realize that the two dolls can both be bathed together in one bath. Pour the jug of water in to the bath, add the bubble bath, and let the children enjoy washing the dolls clean.

Extension

The children could collect water in a water butt or buckets when it rains, and use this to water plants.

Discussion

Discuss all the different uses of water in everyday life for washing, drinking, cooking, brushing teeth, growing plants, etc. Explain how, when there is not much rain, it is especially important not to waste water, so that there will be enough for everyone, eg by sharing baths or showers, always putting plugs in sinks, using cold drinking water from the fridge on hot days, rather than a running tap, and only using the amount you need in kettles and saucepans.

Walk in the dark

Learning opportunities
* Exploring the local environment in the dark, noticing what appears different from during the daytime and helping each other to walk around safely

Links to the Early Learning Goals
* Understanding the world – The world

Equipment and resources
A clear, dry winter's day, warm clothing for everybody, one torch between each two children, fluorescent strips, coloured cellophane, sticky tape, permission slips received from children's parents and carers to allow them to participate in an outing, extra adults to help with supervision.

Activity
Explain to parents and carers that you intend to take the children on a late afternoon winter's walk and invite them to accompany you if they would like to. Attach fluorescent strips to the children's coats with sticky tape and shine a torch onto them, so that the the children can see how they show up in the dark. Discuss the importance of being seen by traffic.

Divide the children into pairs and give each pair a torch. Make sure each adult knows which pair(s) of children he or she is supervising. Walk around the local streets with the children taking turns to use the torch.

Extension

Experiment with covering the torch with coloured cellophane to make everything appear red/green/ blue, etc.

Discussion

During the following day, talk with the children about what might have happened if they had not been able to see where they were walking. Ask whether they know anyone who is blind or partially sighted. Encourage them to remember the sounds they heard and to look in books to find out which animals and birds come out at night. Introduce the word 'nocturnal' and explain what it means and which creatures are nocturnal.

Kind children book

Learning opportunities
* Developing an awareness and an understanding of family history

Links to the Early Learning Goals
* Understanding the world – People and communities

Equipment and resources
Paper, crayons, large sheets of sugar paper, glue, long-armed stapler, sticky tape, photocopier, forms that parents and carers can use to record anecdotes at home and return to the setting for practitioners to use with the group.

Activity
Offer forms to children's parents and carers and suggest that they each write down, at home, a short anecdote about a kind deed that they carried out when they were young. Encourage families to involve grandparents and other family members of that generation too. When the forms are returned to the setting, invite the children to illustrate them, and to stick the original forms and pictures in a large sugar paper book, entitled 'Kind children'. Photographs of the children's parents and grandparents (as children) could also be sent in. Copies of these could be included in the 'Kind children' book.

Extension

Have a special time each day when everyone, children and adults, can talk about anyone who has been kind to them that day.

Discussion

Ask about the children's uncles and aunts and explain that they are the brothers and sisters of their parents. Talk about how the children and their brothers and sisters are kind to each other and how their parents and aunts and uncles were once children together and might have been kind in the same ways.

Around the world week

Learning opportunities
* Developing an awareness and an understanding of diversity and inclusion
* Respecting similarities and differences between people from around the world

Links to the Early Learning Goals
* Understanding the world – People and communities

Equipment and resources
Photocopier, globe or map of the world, display table and board, forms that parents and carers can use to write on at home and return to the setting for practitioners to use with the group.

Activity
Explain to everyone that you intend to celebrate an 'Around the world week' in the setting. Offer forms to children's parents and carers and suggest that they and other family members write down, at home, a favourite, simple recipe (that the children could make), or a simple game, story, song, anecdote or joke from anywhere in the world (with explanatory details, if necessary). During the week, play the games, sing the songs and tell the stories. Make recipes and have tasting sessions for everyone at the end of some sessions.

Extension

The parents' contributions could be made into an 'Around the world' booklet, to be sold to raise money for a children's charity.

Involve the children in designing a display table for the booklets and the items that families may have brought in to show the children. If possible, consider inviting a representative from the chosen children's charity into the setting to talk to the group about how the money they will raise from the sale of the booklet will go to help other people.

Discussion

Find out which countries any of the children have ever visited for a holiday or to see family or friends. Ask whether they have had visitors to stay with them from other countries. Invite them to bring in postcards and other souvenir items to add to the 'Around the world' display.

Get well soon!

Learning opportunities
* Selecting and using a range of materials to design and make a card suitable for a friend who is unwell

Links to the Early Learning Goals
* Expressive arts and design – Exploring and using media and materials

Also
* Understanding the world – Technology
* Literacy – Writing

Equipment and resources
Card, felt-tipped pens, toy catalogues, scissors, craft and recycled materials, a child who is absent due to illness (or someone else that the children know who is not well), tape recorder and blank tape or computer that can send emails.

Activity
Gather the children together and chat to them about the child (or person) who is unwell and their favourite toys, stories or activities. Ask them what they think she might miss while she is not attending the setting (or not participating in her usual activities). Encourage the children to draw or cut out appropriate pictures and add other craft pieces to make a collage on a large piece of folded card. Support children as they write a get well message inside and add 'kisses' and other designs.

Extension

Make a 'cheer-up' tape for the sick child by letting each child record a short message saying what they would like to do with the child when he returns to school/playgroup/ pre-school, etc. If you are unsure of the child (or person) being able to play a tape at home, you could consider writing down the children's messages as they say them and sending them to the home by email, or by post.

Discussion

Ask the children whether they have ever received get well cards, or whether other members of their family sometimes do. Talk about the types of activity that people can do at home when they are not feeling too well, such as jigsaw puzzles, painting and reading.

Look inside

Learning opportunities

* To sing a familiar tune, remembering and using new song words to fit the theme

Links to the Early Learning Goals

* Expressive arts and design – Exploring and using media and materials

Also

* Understanding the world – People and communities

Equipment and resources

Large piece of card, felt-tipped pens.

Activity

On the card draw a row of four vertical ovals, with brown, black, red-orange and yellow-blond hair respectively. Do not draw facial features on the ovals. Beneath the ovals draw four pairs of large eyes – blue, green, brown and grey. Ask the children to hum the tune of 'Baa, Baa Black Sheep', and then teach the words of the following song, pointing to the appropriate hair and eye colours as you sing:

Brown hair, black hair, red hair or blond,
Blue eyes, green eyes, brown or grey,
People may look different on the outside,
But inside they feel just like you!

Extension

Ask the children for ideas for others words that could
be substituted in the song (eg curly hair, straight hair,
long legs, short legs, different clothes, etc).

Discussion

Talk about how people from all over the world
looking different 'on the outside' (having different
features, skin colours and clothes) is what makes
the world so colourful and interesting. Explain
how 'outside' differences do not matter, and are not
important. Say that we all have the same feelings
'on the inside' and should be kind to one another,
otherwise people's feelings can be hurt. Ask the
children to talk about times when they, or a friend,
have had their feelings hurt, and about what we
can all do to cheer someone up to whom this has
happened.

Rubbish gobblers

Learning opportunities
* Designing and making a small litter bin for use in a bedroom
* Understanding the importance of keeping rooms tidy and clean and disposing of rubbish safely

Links to the Early Learning Goals
* Expressive arts and design – Exploring and using media and materials, Being imaginative

Also

* Understanding the world – The world

Equipment and resources
Large pieces of card, felt-tipped pens, paints, crayons, collage items (eg wool, bottle tops, etc), glue, scissors, hole punch, string, parcel tape, rulers, tape measures, plastic-coated wire, small cardboard boxes (donated by children's families if possible).

Activity
Ask children and their families if they could each try to provide a small cardboard box. Tell the children that they can turn their boxes into special 'rubbish gobbler' litter bins to keep their bedrooms tidy, choosing whichever creature they would like for their design (a lion, a tiger, a monster, a robot, etc). Encourage each child to make a 'rubbish gobbler' face on a piece of card. Talk to them about how big their piece of card will need to be, and help them cut out a large mouth, through which the rubbish will be 'fed'. Discuss with

each child the best way of attaching the card to their
bin (eg string, parcel tape, glue or plastic coated wire).

Extension

Ask for ideas for transforming the classroom bins into
'rubbish gobblers'. Take votes on the most popular
suggestions, and involve all the children in designing
the faces for them.

Discussion

Ask the children how they keep their bedrooms
tidy and what sort of rubbish they will put in their
'rubbish gobblers'. Talk more generally about what
would happen if we did not have any litter bins
anywhere.

Made in the USA
Monee, IL
07 July 2026

56549689R00036